Caprice
a stockman's daughter

Nugi Garimara is Doris Pilkington's Aboriginal name. She was born on Balfour Downs Station in the East Pilbara. As a toddler she was removed by authorities from her home at the station, along with her mother Molly Craig and baby sister Anna, and committed to Moore River Native Settlement. This was the same institution Molly had escaped from ten years previously, the account of which is told in *Follow the Rabbit-Proof Fence*.

At eighteen, Doris left the mission system as the first of its members to qualify for the Royal Perth Hospital's nursing aide training program. Following marriage and a family, she studied journalism and worked in film/video production. *Caprice: A Stockman's Daughter*, originally published in 1991, is her first book and won the 1990 David Unaipon National Award. *Follow the Rabbit-Proof Fence* was first published in 1996, and was released internationally in 2002 as the film 'R??-???? Fence,' directed by Phillip Nove?? ??? ?? told in *Under the Wintam??? ???* she was appointed Co-P.? ??? Day Committees' Journe?

Comments on *Caprice*:

"This is a very beautifully written novel. The story begins dramatically and holds reader interests throughout, carried forward by an intelligent and questioning narrative voice."

> Oodgeroo, Jack Davis and Mudrooroo
> Judges of the 1990 David Unaipon Award

"So realistically and simply written that I have to keep reminding myself that it is fiction."

> Susan Perry, *Ballarat Courier*

"There is much that is very painful in the reading of *Caprice*. Yet there is also a tremendous sense of hope and love underlying it all."

> Rod Moran, *National Library of Australia News*

"I was hooked into the story ... I'm already eagerly awaiting her next novel."

> Phillip Everett, Radio 5UV

DORIS PILKINGTON | NUGI GARIMARA

Caprice
a stockman's daughter

University of Queensland Press

First published 1991 by University of Queensland Press
Box 6042, St Lucia, Queensland 4067 Australia
New edition 2002

www.uqp.uq.edu.au

Typeset by University of Queensland Press
Printed in Australia by McPherson's Printing Group

Distributed in the USA and Canada by
International Specialized Book Services, Inc.,
5824 N.E. Hassalo Street, Portland, Oregon 97213–3640

This is a work of fiction and all characters depicted are fictitious.

This project has been assisted by
the Commonwealth Government through
the Australia Council, its arts funding
and advisory body.

Sponsored by the Queensland Office
of Arts and Cultural Development.

Cataloguing in Publication Data
National Library of Australia

Pilkington, Doris, 1937-   .
   Caprice: a stockman's daughter

   I. Title.

A823.3

ISBN 0 7022 3356 0

In the life of an Aboriginal woman, no one is more important than her mother when she is young, her daughters when she is old.

Annette Hamilton
Women's Role in Aboriginal Society

Thanks to my children for their love and support and to Edward for his love, friendship and devotion.

Contents

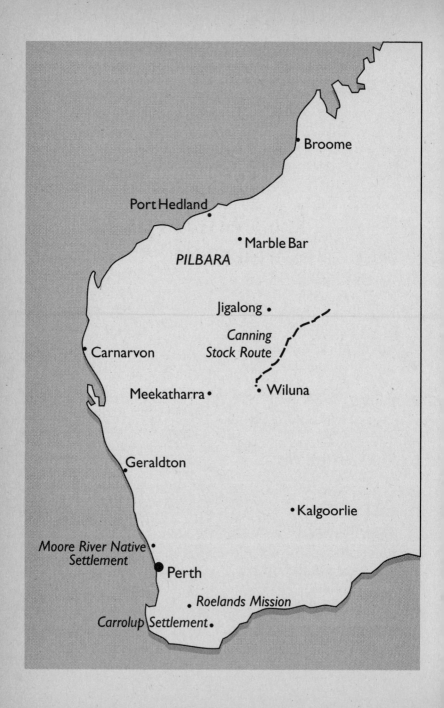

Book 1
Lucy Muldune
1904-1965

Looking For Lucy

The first flush of dawn was appearing in the eastern sky as I entered the cemetery gates. It was heralded by a chorus of birds chirping and twittering as they darted in and out of the grey green spindly mulga trees and clumps of acacia bushes and spinifex grass, pausing only to feed on unsuspecting insects and spiders.

It felt strange and quiet walking alone through a grave-yard at dawn. The only other sounds to be heard at that hour in the morning were the crunch crunching of my sandalled feet on the gravelled road and the buzzing of the scores of bush flies that seemed to appear from nowhere and attach themselves on to any warm blooded living thing that moved from daylight to dusk.

As I approached the graves of my grandparents, Lucy and "Mad" Mick Muldune, daybreak was creeping stealthily across the dry red rugged land, the pinkish golden hues of sunrise forecasting yet another scorching day. As I bent down to place the bouquets of red, white and pink car-nations on their graves, I tried to imagine what they were like and wondered how an Irishman, a bogside lad born a few miles north of the County of Derry, met and married a fullblooded Mandjildjara speaking Aboriginal girl from the remote desert region along the Canning Stock Route in Western Australia. And why did Michael Patrick Joseph

Muldune leave the lush green meadows of Ireland to travel thousands of kilometres across the other side of the world to settle in Kingsley, which must be without a doubt the most arid and certainly the most remote gold mining town in Western Australia. The landscape and the environment contrasted so vastly that it could have been located on another planet.

It didn't matter how deeply I pondered, it was impossible to imagine or even conjure up images and draw sketches of a couple I knew only by name.

That will all change by this evening when I hope to have a full mental picture of them and how they lived. Their headstones are the only tangible evidence I have of their existence. So you see my visit to the graveyard is not a whimsical gesture of a lost soul, nor is it the action of an impulsive insomniac. It is rather a ritualistic performance in a sense, a celebration of a new day; a new beginning. It makes sense to me somehow that my grandparents' final resting place should be the appropriate location to resume my search to establish my true identity. Because their history is my heritage.

●　●　●　●　●

My earlier attempts to trace my roots failed dismally simply because I lacked the knowledge and understanding of Aboriginal culture and traditional "Law". My first mistake was that, being a European-oriented Aborigine, I used the most common approach and from a non-Aboriginal point of view. Naturally, I failed to achieve satisfactory results. Nevertheless, I persisted questioning, but the answers were unchanged. "Your Nanna finished (died) 'long time, your Pop too." Or "Your Pop good Wudgebella (white man) not like some. He look after your Nanna prop'ly. Not use 'em and chuck 'em 'way."

In my ignorance and naivety I expected answers immediately. I expected and assumed that my family would disclose any information and recall any anecdotes and incidents, and be happy to share them with me. I was totally mistaken. Being a family member did not entitle me to any special considerations or privileges.

When I arrived at the Jigalong Aboriginal Community where my grandmother's family came from, approximately 150 kilometres north of Kingsley, I wanted to know and learn everything about my grandparents. However, things didn't go the way I planned. I realised immediately that Jigalong — like other traditionally-oriented communities — had certain codes of social behaviour and social conduct, and more importantly, a belief system that was handed down by super beings of the Dreamtime and commonly referred to as the "Law".

This "Law" includes all religious practices (rites and rituals) and taboos. Members of these communities believe that it is imperative to practise and preserve the "Law". Amongst those taboos is one concerning the aftermath of the death of a family member of the community. When this occurs the name of the deceased must never be used again. Even those having the same sounding name can no longer be called by that name. Persons having the same name as that person are addressed or referred to as "gurnmanu" which simply means "What's his/her name" or "the person who has the same name as the dead one". It is believed that the spirits of the dead become resentful and dangerous so it is customary, at the end of the funeral service, for an elder who knew the deceased well, to say something like "You are dead now, so don't follow us back to the camp. You go straight to your waterhole and leave us alone."

Confused, bewildered, and disappointed, I decided to shelve the project and return home to Geraldton. There was still hope from another source. I needed to find my grandparents' friends, Jack and Phyliss Donaldson. I was confident that I would find them some day, somewhere, somehow.

Well that day has come. At long last I shall be meeting them for the first time here in Kingsley. I can hardly contain my excitement, because I have so many questions to ask them. Questions that have been concealed in my heart for so many years. I want to know about my grandparents' dreams, their aspirations, their hopes, fears and despair. But most of all I am looking forward to travelling back in time — a journey into the past where lie all the answers. The Donaldsons have the golden key that will unlock all the doors and windows to reveal memories, some vivid, others dim and sketchy reflections. This is one day I shall never forget.

Kingsley

I wondered what Michael Muldune's first impressions of Kingsley were, this desolate arid town, population 200-300 fluctuating from time to time. Surely it must have been an impossible place for any white man to settle in. Many preferred to live in the cities or the coastal towns.

In the summer the temperature is between 35°C and 40°C in the shade, the humidity making conditions unbearable. Whirlwinds or willy-willys, those twisting columns of spinifex, red dust and scraps of paper, are seen frequently as they blow through the town.

Dust storms are frequent at certain times of the year. The unwary stranger may look up and see brown and red clouds and mistake them for rain — that is until it comes closer. You certainly know you've been in a sandstorm — it's an experience you'll never forget. These sandstorms have been compared to mini sandstorms of the Sahara Desert.

There's a big panic on when it is sighted. The whole town comes alive and becomes a hive of activity; neighbours warn each other to be prepared for the worst. In a few hours the town will appear to be deserted — the whole population of Kingsley will remain indoors until the storm passes, then the cleaning up operation begins.

The average rainfall is normally between 12 mm and

15 mm and is often uncertain and erratic. Violent thunderstorms are exciting at the onset when the heavy downpour reaches the town. It comes down in torrents. The parched dry land is transformed into a muddy brown red lake in a matter of hours. The creek beds around the town fill to overflowing, spilling their contents across the stony flats. The joyous shouts of excited children echo all over the town as they play in the muddy creeks.

The town of Kingsley was founded by an early explorer named Martin Kingsley in the early 1800s. The Kingsley ranges run north to northwest of the town. In the foreground is the largest creek with the growth of large shady gum trees, some acacia shrubs and spinifex grasses. To the south are dry stony plains, known as gibber plains that reflect the shimmering heat in the hot dry summer months.

The vivid sunsets behind the Kingsley ranges are one of its best features, the brilliant red, oranges, pinks, browns and mauves are something you don't see in the cities and towns in the south of the state.

It was these features and the rugged environment that attracted Mick Muldune, the bogside lad born in a village steeped in tradition and superstition. He was adamant when told of earlier explorers' attempts to introduce the flora and fauna of Europe to this remote part of Western Australia: "You can't change this country with its rugged, tough landscape and make it into the green fields and meadows of Europe," he said. "You have to learn to adapt and live with it, like I have," he told all newcomers to this town, and being an Irishman these were issues he could relate to. He came from a country where bluebells grew thick in the woods of beech, pine, oak, hazel and ash; where hillocks were covered in yellow gorse bushes. His people had a history that went back centuries. From his ancestors he inherited a stubbornness and an unwillingness to be subordinate to colonists who tried to force the original inhabitants to change their lifestyle by destroying their language and culture, then condemning them and persecuting them for being different.

• • • • • •

When "Mad" Mick Muldune arrived in Kingsley he had no special skills but he had a willingness to learn and to do any kind of work available. He wasn't afraid of hard work. So the first thing he did after alighting from the "Old Rattler", the weekly goods train, was to go down to the Kingsley Arms Hotel and enquire after work prospects. "The best place in town to wait. You're sure to find something," the railway workers had assured him.

When he reached the hotel, he met a young man — a lean half-caste seated on the bench outside. This wiry lad was dressed like a local, in white riding breeches, check shirt, high boots and a brown felt hat covering his black curly hair. Mick suddenly felt out of place and uncomfortable in his city clothes — the grey suit, shoes and battered suitcase containing all his worldly goods.

Mick introduced himself to this young stranger and explained his intentions and his reason for being there.

"The same here, I am Jack Donaldson. What sort of work are you looking for?" the young man asked Mick.

"Anything, I'll try anything," Mick replied.

Jack informed Mick that he was waiting to catch the mail truck driven by Bob Brown every fortnight from Kingsley right up to Mitchell's Crossing 600 miles north, calling in on all pastoral stations, or their turnoffs at least, on the way.

"Come with me," suggested Jack, "you never know, we might find something. There's always someone wanting workers, somewhere. You'll need a proper swag though," he added, bending down to touch his own for emphasis, "Like this, see."

Fifteen minutes later Mick had a swag — a blanket roll consisting of a light coconut hair mattress, two unbleached calico sheets, and two bush rugs all rolled up in a canvas ground sheet and tied tightly with binder twine.

Mt Dunbar Station

Seated on old wicker cane chairs on the back verandah, Jack and Phyliss Donaldson told me how it was that my grandfather, Mick Muldune, met my grandmother, Lucy, all those years ago.

• • • • •

The trip on the mail truck was rough and that was putting it mildly. The station roads were some of the most hazardous in the state. After heavy rains, there were washaways — where the roads were washed away. In some places there were no roads but deep creek beds full of running water. Road surfaces changed and varied en route. The traveller could find himself on corrugated gravel roads or potholes full of bulldust, or claypans and loose stones. This form of travel was a new experience for the Irishman. He remained silent throughout the trip north. Was he regretting this impulsive action? thought Jack. I hope not.

They stayed on at Mt Dunbar Station, the first station that wanted workers, for three years, then Jack finished up and went back to Kingsley.

During those three years Mick worked hard and willingly doing all the labour required. There was mustering cattle, cleaning troughs, fixing windmills, boundary riding and breaking in horses. He adapted immediately to station life and liked it.

The owners, Mal and Anne Forbes, had three children, Mark, 10, William, 8, and Caroline, 6.

The Forbes also cared for and provided work for 100 to 200 Aborigines living at "Native Camp", across the other side of the creek from the station. The family clan ranged from able-bodied individuals, children, adolescents and toddlers, to the maimed, lamed and the almost blind old people.

The Forbes, referred to by all the Aborigines as the "boss" and the "missus", lived in a large shady comfortable house called the homestead. The domestic staff consisted of six women who were responsible for the care and the cleaning of the homestead; the duties differed according to age, status and experience. Amongst this group was a young fullblooded Mardu girl called Lucy, a Milangga, who was becoming a favourite of Mrs Forbes because she proved to be reliable, responsive and an excellent worker.

Anne Forbes wasn't the only one who noticed these qualities, apparently.

"I could see that Mick was taking a shine to young Lucy and I tried to talk him out of it," said Jack. "I said to him, 'Wait till we get back to Kingsley and find a nice white woman. Don't marry a fullblood girl'. I was a bit worried the old men might take to him with their spears and boomerangs."

But Mick the Irishman had already made up his mind, he was determined to marry Lucy, this thin straight black-haired girl with a flashing smile and large brown eyes.

From the information he gleaned from "the boss", Mal Forbes, he learned that Lucy had been betrothed to a young man when she was a child, but when she reached marriageable age (thirteen or fourteen) her biljur (promised man) rejected her. His current or first wife did not want to share him with a co-wife.

Mick approached her family and asked for her hand in marriage in the traditional European manner.

He was told by an uncle, the spokesman and tribal elder, "You wait 'til meeting time, big meeting."

These annual "big meetings" usually occurred during the summer months — coinciding with the slack period on all stations in the Murchison and Pilbara regions. This was the time the workers took their holidays.

Certain rites and rituals were performed involving members from other traditionally-oriented communities such as Wiluna, Leonora, Nullagine, Marble Bar, and also others further north.

When the ceremonial rites and rituals were over, meetings discussed the releasing of widows/widowers from mourning period, allowing them to remarry. There were grievances to be aired. Special attention was given to individuals who had disregarded or broken the "Law". These individuals endured physical punishment and social ostracism.

· · · · ·

This kind of deterrent would have to be the most effective I've witnessed, thought Mick nervously.

It was with mixed feeling and trepidation that he joined the group of male elders that morning. He wondered what the hell he was doing there. One white man, a foreigner, an Irishman, surrounded by hundreds of full-blooded Aborigines. He kept his eyes focused on the ground in front of him. He could feel the hundreds of pairs of dark eyes staring silently, boring into his soul.

He definitely would have remained at the station had he not been reassured by his half-caste friend Jack Donaldson that he wouldn't have to become initiated into the Aboriginal tribe to marry Lucy.

"Only tribal boys go through the 'Law'," Jack told him confidently. "Just take your swag, you will camp with the young single fullahs. The old men, the tribal elders, will look after you and tell you what to do. Don't worry it will be alright. You'll see."

Jack advised him well. Mick was instructed where to sit and with whom.

• • • • •

Mick learnt that Dreamtime beings handed down the belief system referred to as the "Law" which included rules for social behaviour, codes and mores of Aboriginal society. The Mardudjara or Mardus (Martus) of the western desert have a unique kinship system which provides a system of moral codes of behaviour, rules for socialisation and marriages. All individuals are categorised into one of four kinship or skin groups, Banaga, Garimara, Burungu or Milangga. Each individual is born into one of these sections and cannot change or transfer into another group. Children are instructed at a very early age to conform to the kinship system, which is very rigid and complicated. The kinship terms are in constant use every day in preparation for more important roles when adulthood is reached. By that stage the pattern of behaviour towards other members of the clan and indeed the community — according to the kinship rules — are established. It is most important that obligations and commitments are fulfilled according to the kinship system.

Lucy, who was in the skin group Milangga, was only allowed to marry a Burungu. A Banaga could only marry a Garimara.

A man must choose a wife from the right section. He cannot marry just any woman of his own choice. The marriage or union can and will be seen as incestuous and can never be accepted by the community. Many couples have eloped only to be apprehended and escorted back to Jigalong to face tribal punishment, which means ostracism and public flogging. These couples ran away to other towns, but one couple went into the desert. They were not followed and brought back like the other lovers, but were left there in self exile and annexation in the Great Sandy Desert.

• • • • •

Mick was given a skin name, Burungu, thus putting him in the appropriate section to be the "right way" or the correct husband for Lucy — a Milangga woman.

With the community's blessings he returned to Kingsley with his intended bride. He returned only once to Jigalong and that was to attend his mother-in-law's funeral.

Although he never accompanied Lucy on her visits to Jigalong, he was content to meet and interact with her relations at the annual race meetings which were held in October and May at the Kingsley race course. There was no pressure on Lucy to abandon or reject her tribal culture or to become involved in ceremonial rites and rituals. She chose the latter. So every year after Christmas, Lucy would spend four to six weeks at Jigalong with her family.

Return to Kingsley

Within a week of the couple's return to Kingsley Mick found employment as a labourer with the Western Australian Government Railways. He tried to talk his mate Jack into applying for a job with him at the Red Hill Mining Company as miners.

"Look, I am a Yamagee, I work on top of the ground — not underneath like a rabbit," Jack said.

"It was only a suggestion," Mick said.

• • • • •

"We should take Katie and show her where her Grannies lived, Jack," suggested Phyliss as she collected our empty mugs.

"Come on then," said Jack, rising from the rickety chair which he picked up and placed in the corner. "We'd better go while it's cool. Leave your ute in the driveway. It'll be safe there."

I'm glad one of us is confident and trusting. I did as I was bid, not completely sure whether I should leave it there. You never know who you cannot trust these days.

Their ancient Holden station wagon had all the characteristics of an outback owner's vehicle — both exterior and interior. I had to move an assortment of tools and mechanical parts to make room for my feet. Everywhere you looked there was red dust about a couple of centimetres thick. I gave a light cough and wound the windows down to let the fresh air in.

"Be careful with that window Katie, sometimes the glass slips down and it's hard to wind up," advised Jack as he started the motor and drove down the main street. He turned right near the Shell garage, stopping only when we came to a couple of pathetic looking tamarisk trees and an equally depressed peppermint tree.

"This is it," said Jack as he pulled up and stopped the engine, and pointed to where the house once stood. It was overrun with couch grass, except in the places where there were concrete slabs.

"This used to be the laundry and the bathroom," he said stamping on them with his right foot for emphasis. "The toilet used to be outside and covered with purple morning glory creepers."

Yes, I could imagine that, quite a common sight even today.

Phyliss plucked a handful of leaves from the miserable looking peppermint tree and crushed them in both hands and took a big sniff. "I used to do this all the time when the old people lived here," she said wistfully.

Jack began pacing up and down, marking an invisible rectangular plot where the bough shed was, or rather where it used to be attached to the front of the house. This was a popular place, often filled with visitors who would come to listen to the Irishman sing or perhaps join in with him.

His Irish tenor's voice would carry across the black stony flats. For a few hours at least, Michael Muldune would be mentally transported to his birthplace in Ireland, borne on wings of song. This was how he was able to express his emotions, through his music.

"Did he talk about his homeland, his country or his family?" I asked wistfully.

"Not much," came the reply from Jack who was trying very hard to recall those memories of yesteryear. "Only that his mother and father, he called them his 'mam' and 'da', died in Ireland, his only sister ran off with a Protestant and that he had an aunt and uncle in America, Boston I think, and some cousins too."

"But surely there must have been times when a memory stirred or he may have had a twinge of nostalgia, perhaps?"

The two old people looked at each other. I could see that they did not quite understand my question so I re-phrased it.

"Did he long for his home, you know, say he wished he was in Ireland at special times of the year?"

"No, but he used to sing a lot when he was feeling low, or miserable. You know all those Irish songs we grew up with," said Jack as he appealed to his memory by cocking his head to one side, at the same time taking a drag on his roll-your-smoke. "You remember, Phyliss, you know, ballads, folksongs and sometimes he had requests from people to sing hymns like 'Beyond the Sunset', 'There is a Green Hill Far Away', and 'Whispering Hope'. But I think his favourite was 'Danny Boy'."

His sentiments were carried pleasantly in the evening, usually at sunset. How many times did he sing this refrain, I wondered. It must have been scores of times during his lifetime, I'd guess.

> But, come ye back, when summer's in the meadow.
> Or when the valley's hushed and white with snow,
> Then I'll be here in sunshine or in shadow,
> Oh, Danny Boy, Oh Danny Boy I love you so.

Lucy never joined in the singing. She preferred to listen to her husband, sometimes humming silently to herself.

"Your grandfather leased this block from the railways and when he died they reclaimed it," said Jack, marking the invisible boundary with his right hand.

"Well we'd better go back before it gets too hot," said Phyliss, this gentle gracious little half-caste lady who had befriended my grandmother so many years before.

I was reluctant to leave this place. I wanted to spend a few more minutes and try to visualise and feel their ghostly presence as they must have sat in the shady bough shed shooing the sticky bush flies away from their meals and themselves. This is where they sat silently or singing, but always watching the vivid sunsets every evening — a different one each day, none the same, special uninhibited views of the beautiful Kingsley sunsets.

The Donaldsons

Jack Donaldson began work immediately on his return from Mt Dunbar Station, as an orderly at the Kingsley Hospital.

"I liked it until they asked me to do a shift in the morgue, you know, handling dead people. I couldn't do that, I told the matron, Matron O'Neil," he said.

"I told them I was pulling out straight away. But they called me back and gave me a job as the gardener," he said proudly, his leathery sunburnt face lighting up with self-satisfaction.

Phyliss Charles was one of the hospital laundresses. Her Auntie Bella Charles was the senior laundress. Their working day began at 5.00 am, lighting the two coppers. They washed everything by hand — no washing machines in those days.

"We starched and ironed the next day. We worked really hard then," remembered Phyliss.

Phyliss actually came up from Geraldton for a holiday with her aunt and decided to stay on in Kingsley.

"I'm glad she did, cos I wanted to marry her as soon as I set eyes on her," said Jack.

She was a very attractive young girl, short — not quite five feet — slightly plump with dark brown hair, not too curly, but nice and wavy. She was a pleasant smiling, popular young woman. She and Jack were married six months later at Geraldton.

At the same time, Lucy was working as a part-time kitchen hand, until she became pregnant with Peggy, who became my mother.

"Mad" Mick Muldune

Before Lucy and Mick Muldune were married, Sergeant Andrew (Andy) Miller and other white people in town tried to undermine their relationship and some even went as far as encouraging unattached white women to seduce the Irishman.

"Marry a nice white woman," they said.

There were few white eligible women to choose from: there were the nurses from the hospital, the local barmaids and a few transients, so the competition amongst the men folk of the town was fierce. The ratio must have been in the vicinity of 80:1. There must have been more unmarried males in Kingsley than anywhere else in Western Australia.

"We used to watch all the young white fullahs, all spruced up, going up the path to the nurses' quarters to try their luck," said Jack grinning sardonically.

The Irishman used to tell the others, "Why should I want to marry a white woman when Lucy's perfect for me. She doesn't yell or shout and let her tongue run away out of control.

"And further," he added, "When I go out I know she'll be waiting for me at home.

"No man, and I mean no man," getting quite angry now, "will covet my wife. I can trust her not to run away with any oily-tongued, charming hawker."

Is this what happened to the Irishman back in his homeland? Did a hawker elope with his sweetheart? Perhaps so, or perhaps not. Who knows? He was a very private person, secretive and selective. No one will ever know. He continued expounding Lucy's attributes with great fervour.

"She's a good cook, a good housekeeper. She's not a demanding, domineering woman. She suits me very well, thank you very much."

To Mick Muldune, Lucy compared with his mother as the embodiment of pure womanhood. A most unusual comparison considering one was an Aborigine and one was Irish. "Me mam was a saint, who struggled all her life without complaining. God bless her."

Others tried to influence him by attacking Lucy personally, advising him, "You don't have to marry her. Do what the other white men do."

"Oh, and what's that," snapped Mick, getting angry and annoyed with these so-called well-meaning friends.

"Stay with these gins until a decent white woman comes along," said another boring condescending man.

"Are you saying that Lucy is not a decent woman?" roared Mick, who was moving menacingly towards him, his large fists clenched ready to strike.

"No! No, I didn't mean that at all Mick," said the man backing slowly away from the bar.

"I am making Lucy my wife and that's that," said Mick with finality. All discussion on the matter stopped abruptly.

• • • • •

Was my grandfather really mad? I wondered. Because to describe him as "mad" would be to attribute insane qualities such as spontaneous violence, wouldn't it?

I was reassured by the Donaldsons that although he

frequently dished out his own form of Irish deterrent, "he wasn't mad in the head".

"And he didn't always win either," said Jack passionately as he recalled dimmed memories. "I seen him get flogged a couple of times."

Sergeant Andy Miller, the sandy haired officer in charge of the Kingsley police station, was a large strong and powerful man.

"He must have been about 24 stone, a real big man," said Jack.

"In fact, he looked like those policemen in cartoons. You know those big-chested blokes like that," Jack said, spreading his arms wide.

He didn't ignore Mick's behaviour — especially when a pugilist like him metes out his own form of punishment. That's taking the law into his own bare hands; or rather his large bare knuckles. It was impossible to reassure some that the Irishman wasn't mad. His fines amounted to a few bob.

Mick Muldune always maintained that he fought to uphold his principles and he was ready to defy the law for them. But he never made moral judgment on any man.

Under normal circumstances he was the most law-abiding citizen, and one of the most civic minded. He was by birth a fervent Catholic, so naturally enough blasphemy against the Pope and the Catholic church, also racism and bigotry, would rile him.

But there were two things he hated with a firmly ingrained vehemence: they were the colonists and the constabulary.

This became apparent one Saturday afternoon when the public bar at the Kingsley Arms Hotel was full to capacity, and the topic was marriage ceremonies. This incident occurred before Mick and Lucy were married.

"The sergeant has powers vested in him to perform

marriages, funerals and things, you know, anything legal," informed a stranger at the other end of the bar.

"What!" roared "Mad" Mick the Irishman, "me get married by the local constabulary!

"Jesus, Mary, Joseph, me mam and da will roll over in their graves. Holy Mother of God. What blasphemy," he moaned.

He turned to face the unfortunate stranger and continued to bombard him with verbal abuse, pausing only to glare at him with contempt.

"How dare you suggest such a thing," he said, banging his large fist on the bar top, making the drinkers grab their glasses firmly in their hands. He apparently took a quick sip from his glass of beer and without wiping the froth from his mouth, he continued his verbal attack on the stranger.

"Well," recalled Jack, "some of the blokes in the pub saw the white froth around his mouth and passed the word around that the Irishman was frothing at the mouth like a mad dog with rabies."

"I only made a suggestion," said the stranger meekly. He was visibly agitated and bewildered by my grandfather's outburst. This surely was a reaction he never expected.

"He was a miner from the Red Hill Mine, southeast of the town, there wasn't as many slag dumps as there is now. He left quicker than he came in. Poor bugger," said Jack sardonically.

Someone made a drunken, submissive speech, and thus pacified the Irishman and everything went back to normal, well almost normal. Many were still astonished and confused by Mick's outburst. They couldn't understand it at all.

"That's why they called him 'Mad' Mick or the 'Mad Irishman' — though not to his face, mind you. They wouldn't be game enough," said Jack.

The Wedding Day

"Mick and Lucy were married by Father John Delvany," said Jack. "The marriage ceremony took place in Matron Margaret O'Neil's sitting room. I was best man and Phyliss was Lucy's matron-of-honour. We had drinks and eats after. Most of the hospital staff and railway workers came to their wedding."

Mick and Lucy lived simply and quietly by themselves without any interference from anyone and were very devoted to each other. Lucy's patience and silence bothered many visitors.

"They thought she was deaf and dumb because she didn't talk much in those days," said Phyliss.

"I got sick of telling them that was the way with tribal women and also that she was very shy when strangers were about.

"The only time I saw her get wild was when she was carrying (pregnant) for your mother Peggy," said Phyliss quietly.

"Yeah, I remember that time," smiled Jack. "He forgot to bring some oranges and tinned lambs tongues home for her.

"She banged a pot on the table and swore in Mardu Wangka, her own lingo. I don't know what she called him. Well I never seen that Irishman move so quickly.

" 'Sorry, dear, I forgot,' he said sheepishly and he hurried down the road to the store."

Their relationship was truly established; their marriage flourished with few demands made on each other, which resulted in less pressure and tension. They accepted each other for what they were. They never tried to change or act out roles, and they never got on each others nerves. Mick often said, "You can't expect respect and tolerance from others if you have none yourself."

Despite her husband's reputation as a pugilist who violently thrashed the daylights out of abusive, insulting and offensive men, he never showed any violence towards Lucy.

Although she was not demonstrative with her affection for her husband — the embracing and touching, the natural displays of love — her facial expressions and smiles said all. Her emotions were not suppressed but merely simmering under the surface, and remained hidden from prying eyes. This was yet another aspect of their unique relationship and a new quality Mick Muldune saw in his young wife to whom he vowed "to love and cherish, until death do us part".

Book 2
Peggy Muldune
1922-1940

The Thunderstorms

It was late afternoon, the humidity was making the conditions most unbearable.

"Isolated thunderstorms, that's what it said on the hospital wireless last night," said Phyliss as she gazed expectantly towards the north, beyond the gorges and breakaway country — as if she was willing the rolling clouds to move faster and empty their contents on this arid thirsty town.

The two friends could hear the thunder clouds rumbling in the distance. "The storm might get here about suppertime," predicted Phyliss hopefully.

"Yes, might be suppertime, he come," agreed Lucy, nine months pregnant and extremely uncomfortable and restless. She was seated on a single bed in the bough shed. Phyliss and Jack Donaldson's eighteen month old son Michael John lay asleep on the bed opposite.

"You alright Lucy?" asked her friend with a slightly worried expression on her face. "Can't you rest today? You know what Matron O'Neil and Dr Callahan said, 'Get plenty of rest.' "

It was impossible to relax. Even the black iron stones across the flats were shimmering in the heat, making it worse by reflecting the midsummer heat.

"I'll be glad when the sun goes down," sighed Phyliss. "At least it will be a little bit cooler for us."

Lucy said nothing but nodded in agreement. She was absolutely sick of her condition. Big and fat. Can't walk around much. Never mind, she thought to herself — soon be over — everything. The prospect pleased her greatly. Not long now, she smiled softly.

About 5:00 in the afternoon there was a loud clap of thunder followed by flashes of lightning. Excitement and peals of laughter came from the houses behind them, accompanied by shouts of expectancy, "Yore, yore!"

The two friends had spent months cutting out and sewing a layette for the baby. There was still plenty of calico left to make more matinee jackets and nappies as the baby grew and developed.

Raindrops on the roof? The women pricked up their ears. Then it came down, the heavy, powerful torrents of rain came to give them relief. The frightening loud, unusual noise had woken Michael John who began howling in fear. His mother picked him up and tried to pacify her frightened son.

"Phyliss, my baby, he coming now," said Lucy.

"Oh, my God," blurted the panic-stricken friend, holding her own child closer to her chest. "You take Michael John, while I go over the road and get Clarry Pincher," said Phyliss as she raced out into the storm.

"Lucy's ready to go to the hospital, will you take her?" Phyliss was dripping wet but that was the least of her worries right now.

"Clarry's car was one of those square things — olden day cars. Worth a lot of money nowadays," informed Jack.

"He took us to the Kingsley Hospital and dropped us off then drove to the railway yards to tell Mick," said Phyliss.

Phyliss stayed with her friend until Matron O'Neil and Dr Callahan came into the labour ward, then she went in search of her husband the hospital gardener. The couple drove home in their brown run-about.

Water was everywhere, like a large lake — the creeks were filled to overflowing. What a lovely sight — most welcome indeed. The sight of it made the locals feel cooler.

The Donaldsons had an early supper then sat in the bough shed to watch the storm and wait for news of the birth of baby Muldune.

"Your grandfather came home about one o'clock in the morning looking like a drowned rat. His black hair was straight and dripping wet," said Jack.

"He had the biggest grin on his face. Yeah the biggest I ever saw."

"It's a girl! It's a girl! We're calling her Margaret Bridgid Muldune, Margaret after Maggie O'Neil and Bridgid after me mam," he said excitedly.

She weighed 6lb 5oz and she was beautiful, the proud father told them. The resemblance was remarkable. He was perfectly satisfied that Peggy — that was what he called her — was the most wonderful gift in the whole wide world. He doted on her from her birth and continued to dote on his only child throughout the following years.

The Tragedy

Despite her mixed parentage, Peggy did not feel different from other children. She was certainly a fortunate child, never subjected to racial discrimination or prejudice. She attended the normal state school when other Aboriginal children were denied access. She completed six primary levels and two secondary grades, and did exceptionally well in all grades. It was widely acknowledged that the coaching and the extra tutoring from her godparents, Dr John Callahan and his wife, Matron Margaret Callahan (nee O'Neil) had been largely responsible for the high standard produced by the only half-caste pupil at the Kingsley Government School.

Everything was going perfectly wonderfully for this pretty teenager with long straight black hair and large green eyes, features inherited from her Irish father.

Matron Callahan discussed the future prospects for Peggy with her parents: nursing training at the Royal Perth Hospital, she suggested. Peggy would stay with the Callahans in South Perth. Lucy objected strongly. She didn't mind her working as a ward's maid or a nurse's assistant at the Kingsley Hospital. But send her away to Perth — definitely not.

It was a week after Peggy's fourteenth birthday that the tragedy struck the Muldune family. An accident at the railway yards cut Mick Muldune's life short. They said it was a freak accident, the concrete pipes had rolled off the back of a truck and on to him and crushed his ribcage and stomach. He died on the way to the hospital. The pipes narrowly missed two other men. They said they yelled out for him to "Look out", but he never heard them. He went quickly to his tragic end.

Michael Patrick Joseph Muldune, known affectionately as the "Irishman" or "Mad" Mick, was laid to rest in the Kingsley Cemetery. Many mourners like Jack Donaldson, his best friend and best man, stood mute, tears coursing unashamedly down their cheeks.

Jack was silently remembering the Muldunes' wedding day, fifteen years ago. Lucy dressed in a pink linen two-piece suit, white blouse and hat while Phyliss her matron-of-honour in an identical pale blue suit. Jack and Mick were dressed in dark navy pin-striped suits and white shirts — but no ties. "We joked about that, the Irishman and me. We never owned a tie. The Irishman promised he would buy one and wear it at the funeral — whoever went first. He's wearing the same clothes he wore at his wedding, on his wedding day — but with a brand new black tie."

A nudge from Phyliss bought him back to earth abruptly.

"Bye my Irish friend, I'll remember you always," sobbed this tall sunburnt half-caste Aboriginal man, before turning away to walk back towards his ute. They said that Mick Muldune stood for justice, honesty and fair play.

His widow Lucy and daughter did not leave Kingsley immediately. There were other formalities to be taken care of — according to Aboriginal custom. All Mick's personal possessions were taken out to the backyard by female relations and burnt, nothing was saved except three beautiful crochet rugs — these were rescued by Peggy herself. All personal papers, records gone. The house itself was smoked out with Lucy and Peggy and other close relatives inside — a cleansing ritual, leaving nothing familiar for the spirit of her husband to find and cling to. He will find his own resting place — his own waterhole as it were.

Mt Dunbar Station Revisited

Lucy and Peggy settled into station life quietly and comfortably. Nothing had changed, the routine remained the same, unchanged since the establishment of the pastoral station in the early 1900s.

Peggy became the companion to Patricia Forbes, the "boss's" fourteen year old daughter. She was glad too. She didn't have to live in the "camp", the "Native Camp" across the creek where over a hundred Aboriginal people lived. Their homes were built of cast off sheets of iron, one-roomed with a bough shed of wire netting on two sides and on the roof. There was no running water. Water was carried in four-gallon drums from a tap fifty yards away.

The people at the camp suffered as a result of the unhygienic conditions. The poor nutrition and the lack of fresh fruit and vegetables in their diet contributed to complaints such as malnutrition, chest infections, trachoma, and infected ears.

The usual weekly station rations for the camp contained: 3 bags of flour, 2 bags of sugar, 6 packets of tea, 4 tins of jam, 2 tins of golden syrup, 2 tins of treacle, 4 tins of milk, 2 tins of curry powder, 4 packets of rice, 6 plugs of tobacco, pieces of salted beef, and occasionally fresh beef. To supplement this station-introduced food, the people camped out every weekend and lived on traditional "bush tucker" cooked in the traditional way. This was one thing Peggy enjoyed, going out with the old people to forage for minyara (wild onion) and kulyu (wild yams).

She liked the winter days here. The clear bright warm, sort of lazy, days. This is the time when the honey flowers are out. These bunches of golden yellow flowers are collected from the desert oaks. The nectar from these flowers is shaken into the palms of the hands or soaked in a bucket of water to make a sweet refreshing drink.

All the game caught was cooked in hot ashes. Peggy agreed that this was the only way "bush tucker" should be cooked and eaten. She really looked forward to the weekends — if only for the chance to camp out under the stars. The night sky seemed brighter somehow, and the stars bigger. This was certainly the part of Aboriginal culture she enjoyed the most.

One thing she could not understand. "Why do the old people keep all those dogs?" she asked her mother. Some were alright, but a few of them were the mangiest dogs she ever saw.

"The old people always had a lot of dogs. They tell them if anyone, you know, stranger fullahs, come close to camp," explained Lucy.

"They tell the old people if 'dgingarbil', feather foot man, come too close," said Lucy. "Dginagarbil are mans who chase and kill people who break Mardu Law. They move nighttime in the dark."

In the summer months Patricia and Peggy rode to the various windmills around the property to swim in the windmill tanks or the small pools in the surrounding creeks. The girls were inseparable.

During the milder weather when the wild flowers were in full bloom the pair packed picnic lunches and rode to different locations each time so that Peggy could enjoy the seasonal changes.

Lucy was justly proud of her seventeen year old daughter. She had grown into a beautiful woman, reminding her so much of Mick. Only yesterday she had a very private talk with "the missus" and asked her to act as matchmaker to find a suitable husband for Peggy.

"I don't want a Mardu (fullblood) boy to marry with my daughter," said Lucy, her voice barely audible, fearing others may overhear her conversation with Mrs Forbes. Everyone, including Dr and Matron Callahan, Mal and Anne Forbes, convinced Lucy that her beautiful intelligent daughter deserved much better, by their standards obviously. Lucy's own marriage had been both enriching and fulfilling and she imagined and hoped for the same for her only daughter, Peggy.

"I want Muda, Muda (half-caste) boy — same as my girl — you know, one read and write, or a good Wudgebella (white man) — not Mardu," she added quietly.

Mrs Forbes promised to help. Mrs Forbes was in regular contact with women on neighbouring stations who could have suitable half-caste station hands working on their properties. She would begin by contacting other stations and making discreet inquiries over the pedal set (wireless/radio).

Lucy's Auntie Minda, a bad tempered old lady, admonished her for letting "the missus" try to make Peggy into a Wudgebella Wandi (white girl).

"You bring 'em back to camp. This place here," she said, pounding the ground with her warda (digging stick) for emphasis, "and sit down (stay) here."

Her high pitched, loud, rasping voice was heard all over the camp. This is another custom. Individuals are encouraged to exercise this right. This prevents any spreading of malicious gossip. There is no room for secretiveness in a traditional Aboriginal community. Meetings are called where everyone attends, either to listen and learn or to participate, whatever the case may be.

"We don't want Peggy to go 'nother way (with strangers to a strange land or place) and lose 'em for good (go away and not return), " said Auntie Minda.

Unaware of the concern she had caused down at the camp, Peggy had ridden out with Patricia towards the old copper mine to the windmill to meet Colin Morgan, the station's white overseer, and his black offsider, Danny (Dinnywarra) Atkinson. The clay pans were still filled with water and all around them, especially under the mulga trees, the normally red earth was covered in a carpet of pink, white, yellow and mauve flowers.

"This is what makes station life so special," said Patricia proudly. "The wide open spaces, the stony ridges and the dry red dusty plains.

"For months all you see is the burnt looking country. Then after a good rainfall, it changes into this," stretching her arms.

"I can't imagine living anywhere else! When I was away at boarding school in Perth I really missed this place."

A few miles south, Auntie Minda's husband Jimbo was out boundary riding, searching for and rounding up stray cattle and driving them closer to the nearest windmill. As he approached the windmill he spotted smoke rising from the creek. This gladdened his heart. He hadn't had a decent feed for a couple of days — fresh beef and damper washed down with hot sweet tea will go well, he thought. With visions of food he spurred his mount faster.

But when Jimbo reached the creekbed, he didn't like what he saw. He couldn't believe his eyes. It was not as he supposed, the two girls picnicking nearby, for what he saw was a trysting place for young lovers. Patricia Forbes, the boss's daughter, was seated on a blanket in the shade of a big river gum, very close to Colin Morgan. A little further to the right were Danny and Peggy. A Burungu and a Garimara. Alarmed at this sight before him and of the dangerous position those two young people had placed themselves in, he shook his head in disbelief.

"That's wrong way, this can't be. Not right, not right," he said.

What was Peggy thinking of. There was no excuse, she knew the consequences for breaking rules — especially becoming involved with a man of the wrong skin. This was a serious offence. Since her thirteenth birthday she was said to have been endowed with wisdom beyond her years, so she was well aware that this rendezvous, and more importantly the chance of discovery, meant physical punishment for both of them.

So what made her disregard and flout the "Law"? Was it just the love of adventure or was it just sheer youthful abandonment that got the better of her discretion and good judgment? I think not. I think Peggy was a romantic who was passionately in love with Danny even though he was a Burungu, and she was simply enjoying the youthful pleasures of love and excitement.

Jimbo rode on — unseen by the young lovers who were obviously far more interested in each other than their beautiful surroundings — to pass this information on to Lucy.

Lucy was absolutely furious. "Why did my girl have to shame me like this!" She clenched and unclenched her fists and threw her hands up in the air with despair. "Why? Why?" She watched and simmered all afternoon.

"That Danny, he's the one. He's the big trouble maker." She went on in this vein for the rest of the day, blaming Danny for seducing her beloved and only daughter.

Patricia and Peggy arrived home unaware that their

picnic had created an incident that was about to erupt like a volcano with effects just as far reaching.

The girls showered and changed into cool looking shorts and blouses, then sat relaxing on the verandah. A few seconds later, their peace and quietness was shattered. A very irate and fuming Lucy stormed on to the verandah and grabbed her daughter by her long black hair and dragged the screaming, frightened girl outside, then proceeded to beat her across the back and shoulders with a long warda (digging stick), the same one she would use on Peggy's lover.

"Mum! Dad!" screamed Patricia in fear and alarm for her companion, "Come quickly, Lucy's gone mad!"

Mal Forbes grappled with Lucy who seemed at this moment to be transformed into an extremely strong mad woman. He removed the offensive weapon and calmly asked for an explanation for this unusual display of violence.

Yes, quite out of character for Lucy, thought Anne Forbes. This must be serious. She led Lucy out to the shadehouse and waited for her to settle down and control herself. Lucy then explained quietly what had happened. Mrs Forbes said confidently, "I agree Peggy should be taken from the influences of the native (fullblood) men. She's too good for the likes of them." She helpfully suggested that Peggy be sent to the Moore River Native Settlement, north of Perth, where all the half-caste children and young people were trained and educated in skills that would be useful to them when they entered the wider community.

"There would be a better selection of young men, more suitable for a girl like Peggy," said Mrs Forbes.

But once again Lucy's hopes and desire to control her daughter's destiny were thwarted. For during those brief encounters Peggy shared with her lover, a spiritual affection between the two was born; an affinity which lasted till her death. No other love could replace that.

Patricia finally pacified her friend, then went out to the shadehouse to speak to her mother. Mrs Forbes and Lucy were seated in the coolest spot, talking softly and rationally now. Not realising the seriousness of the situation, Patricia pleaded and begged them not to send Peggy away. Her tearful pleadings fell on deaf ears, for the decision had been made.

Lucy rose from the chair and walked sadly towards the door.

"Send 'em Peggy down to my camp, I can watch 'em all the time. Can't run around," asked Lucy.

At the camp, voices were raised, abuses, insults were hurled back and forth. Lucy took her warda and flayed into Danny. Other members of the clan followed suit.

Early the next morning, before sunrise, a very sore and bruised Danny was taken by his parents in a horse and cart back home to Jigalong.

The following week Lucy and a very distraught Peggy who had to be forced into the back of the mail truck, still weeping unrestrainedly, travelled to Kingsley.

• • • • •

Sgt Andy Miller was pleasantly surprised when he met the mail truck that evening. Here was a beautiful seventeen year old woman with slightly waved jet black hair hanging to her shoulders. When she looked up there was no mistaking those beautiful green eyes just like "the Irishman". The only thing different from her father was her light olive skin.

It wasn't so long ago, well it didn't seem that long, when he and others having a drink at the Kingsley Arms had tried to persuade Mick not to marry Lucy but wait for a more suitable woman, preferably a white one.

And now here was Lucy taking real drastic steps to prevent her own daughter from marrying a man she considered unsuitable. Tomorrow morning she would travel by train hundreds of miles southwest to the Moore River Native Settlement. It seemed like history was repeating itself.

A week later mother and daughter arrived at their final destination, the Moore River Native Settlement.

Eight months later Peggy Muldune gave birth to a healthy six pound baby girl with thick black hair and large dark brown eyes. As she held her baby in her arms, she said weakly, "Her name is Katherine Bridgid Muldune, but call her Kate." This was the only time all three Muldune women were together. Twenty-four hours later Margaret Bridgid Muldune was dead. The sister-in-charge of the hospital told Lucy that her daughter died of "the fever". But her friends and workmates said she died of a broken heart, in other words she just pined away for the handsome young Aboriginal stockman with curly sun-bleached hair and flashing smile, the man she left on Mt Dunbar Station, hundreds of miles northeast of the Settlement, a place she was destined never to see again.

• • • • •

Lucy went back to Kingsley bereft of her most precious possessions, her beloved husband and her beautiful daughter, and spent the rest of her days living with her cousin Daisy. In the late afternoons on most days, someone would find her in the backyard, a tragic figure standing motionless, staring silently at the slope on the gravelled hillside, her dark eyes filled with sadness and despair. She seldom smiled.

Some people even say that my grandmother gave up living when my mother and grandfather died. She was the epitome of sorrow and grief, until she passed away one hot summer night, in her sleep. She was buried next to her husband, the Irishman who sang sentimental songs about his homeland, of "watching the sun go down in Galway Bay", and of the sun "declining beneath the blue sea" and of "valleys hushed and white with snow".

It seemed so bizarre and yet so poignant. Tears welled up in my eyes and spilled down my cheeks, and through the veil of tears I could see the hillslope with its rows of white crosses and realised that there was just one thing left to do before I returned to Geraldton.

Ten minutes later I stood alone once more beside their graves. This time it was to share an experience with them. And that was to watch the sun sink slowly behind the rugged Kingsley Ranges. I like to think that this is exactly where they want to be — this unlikely couple by divine intervention will remain side by side on this gravelled slope on the hillside watching all the beautiful sunsets for evermore.

The togetherness they shared in life is continuing in death.

Book 3
Kate Muldune-Williamson
1940-

Moore River Native Settlement

When the Moore River Native Settlement was opened in 1918, it was to have been the ideal environment where half-caste children would receive basic education and be trained in semi-skilled jobs. The inmates present at the beginning were brought down from stations in the north under ministerial warrants and confined against their will in this strange place amongst strangers. For these children — many just toddlers not yet weaned from their mothers' breasts — this was no doubt the most traumatic experience in their young lives, and even more so for their bewildered mothers, grandmothers and other relatives left behind to grieve.

The wailing and the mourning went on for a long time — until time and tears wiped out all memories of their lost children. Many mothers never saw their children again. They were discouraged from visiting them, in case these visits would disturb the children and interfere with their education. Even in the Settlement the mothers were segregated from their children. This government institution was a residential school for part-Aboriginal or half-caste children only. Non-Aboriginal staff were employed, as well as the older boys and girls who were later sent away to work on stations. The Settlement also housed unmarried mothers and their babies. About 300 yards away was the "camp" where Aboriginal families lived. Many were former inmates who had moved back to the area to send their children to the Settlement school.

Mr A.O. Neville, Chief Protector of Aborigines (1915-1940) saw this scheme as a positive move towards a final solution of the part-Aboriginal "problem". The inmates would be encouraged to seek marriage partners from white or near-white individuals. He envisaged that this policy, based on controlled racial inter-marriages, would eventually lead to a gradual "breeding out" of Aboriginal genes.

However the administrators and indeed the government of the day overlooked one important factor, and that was that for an experiment of this kind to succeed an ideal environment for this new Aboriginal society must be created — one where total segregation was essential. The children had to have no physical contact with any Aboriginal adult if they were to become the clones or hybrids that Mr Neville and his policy makers hoped to produce.

Fortunately for these children they had at least some interaction and contact with adults even if it was under controlled conditions. These adults were the nurse maids, cooks, laundresses and surrogate mothers at the Settlement. Breast-feeding motherless babies was a common practice amongst nursing mothers. Baby Kate Muldune was one of many babies who was loved and nurtured by her aunt Josie Leach, mother of Kevin John born a couple of days before her.

On arrival at the Settlement the newcomers were told that speaking "native language" was forbidden. Those who misunderstood or knowingly disobeyed the instruction (which had become an unwritten law) and continued to communicate in their traditional language were intimidated and victimised by others. Foreign and colonial words such as "uncivilised", "primitive" and "savages" were bandied about in the compound and the school playground.

This was a form of subtle indoctrination based on fear and superstition that gave birth to one of the damaging concepts in this so-called new Aboriginal society — discrimination against their own people.

With their mothers, grandmothers and other blood relations behind an invisible wall of silence and obscurity, all traces of their existence vanished. All links to their traditional, cultural and historical past were severed forever.

No one imagined or perceived at that time what repercussions and effects this would have on future generations, and what a fatal impact it would have on the Aboriginal people of Western Australia who were deprived of their history and their values. These light-skinned institutionalised, ruralised people were living under what we know now to be a misconception that they were superior to their fullblooded relations, whom they despised and were ashamed to own. This proved that the indoctrination and conditioning had succeeded on one level at least. These half-caste or part-Aboriginal children would never choose a husband or wife whose skin colour was darker than theirs.

All memories of the past will be forgotten. Rejection of their own culture is permanent. The process of reshaping their lives has just begun. They will become children and indeed persons with no past, the new people of tomorrow, the new breed of children to be known as the Settlement kids.

The Compound

In 1947, Kate Muldune was seven, old enough to start school, so she was transferred to the schoolgirls dormitory. The kindergarten had been her home since she was two years old. It cared for all the children aged six years and under and the conditions there were better than anywhere else on the Settlement. The food was adequate: pots of soups and stews, daily supply of milk, dried or tinned fruit and tinned vegetables. The children thrived on the loving care given by the white sister-in-charge and her dedicated staff. The children were doted on and cuddled often, no one missed out. Kate still remembers the smell of Lifebuoy Soap at bath-times.

The schoolgirls dormitory was an overcrowded, dilapidated, vermin-infested building. The beds were covered with mattresses filled with coconut hair or husks, no sheets, just government-issued rugs. At night the beds were pushed closely together, the older girls at the ends protecting their younger relatives in the middle. During the winter, spare mattresses were thrown over the blankets for extra warmth.

"The big girls told us that the dormitory was built on a cemetery or an old yard, and that every night ghosts wandered around the dormitory seeking revenge on the violators of sacred ground," said Kate.

"If we wanted to go to the toilet bucket at night, a small fire of coconut husks or fibre was lit. Still you glanced nervously around before you sat down over the bucket," she added.

The girls were locked in every evening at six o'clock and confined there until sunrise the next morning.

"The food was terrible. The watery stews were made from mutton or sausages that tasted slightly off, with un-sliced cabbage leaves floating on top, potatoes and some-times carrots," said Kate pulling an ugly face. "Weevilly porridge was sweetened with molasses or sugar if it was available. There was at least one redeeming factor, and that was there was always plenty of hot fresh bread, baked daily at the bakehouse, and of course big mugs, or in our cases fruit or Nestles milk tins, of sweet tea. The same fare was served daily and seldom varied.

"You ate the food served to you or you starved, and you said grace before you sat down to eat a meal.

"It was always the same prayer, 'For what we are about to receive may the Lord make us truly thankful. Amen.'

"What I hated most and it always makes me want to puke when I think about it, sometimes we had tinned fruit and custard. Custard indeed, it looked and tasted like lemon coloured glue. Yuk," said Kate looking positively ill.

The girls were awakened at 5:30am rain, hail or shine. After breakfast they bathed and dressed for school. Most of the children enjoyed attending classes in the two-roomed school. The infant school (pre-primary) was attached to the kindergarten. Their teacher was Miss Chapman, a slightly built lass with short curly brown hair. Miss Hillman, a very large middle-aged woman with very short curly grey hair, was also the headmistress who taught upper levels (standards 3-8), while a sturdy, spry Yorkshire woman, a Mrs Brinkley, took the lower primary levels (standards

1-3). Mrs Brinkley's class sat at long oaken desks — four to a desk — with individual inkwells.

"I had the most difficult time — I suppose the same as many of my classmates, trying to write with a pen and ink," said Kate. "I don't know how many times I got hit across the knuckles, with a command to 'hold it straight'. They gave up in disgust. 'Kate Muldune you'll never learn,' they said.

"I hated the bloody pens, I am glad we have biros now."

The availability of a formal education was seen by inmates not as a privilege but as a right, one to replace the birthright that was taken away from them. All the children looked forward to school because it was a place where pupils could forget their degrading living conditions and their horrible meals and concentrate on more important and far more interesting subjects. Apart from the three Rs there were stories to be heard, stories not about Dreamtime heroes, but about the European heroes such as William Tell, Robin Hood, the Scarlet Pimpernel and others. There were tales of the adventures of "Black Beauty", "Robinson Crusoe" and "Treasure Island" and more. Myths and legends of foreign countries replaced the mythical beings of their traditional culture.

Now their mythical beings had names like fairies, elves, witches, goblins and hobyahs. These appeared to be more real to the children because there were colourful pictures of them in many of the books available at the school. Kate's education was constantly expanding.

The standard of education was equal to all other state or government schools in Western Australia. This was indicated by requests from the school inspector Mr Thornton for samples of work done by pupils at the Settlement school. The pupils were being groomed to become "model citizens" to be placed in positions of responsibility that would enable them to take their places in any level of society — or so they were told.

The school was the venue for all social functions, such as the monthly dances for the adults from the compound and the camps. The children watched on with delight as the old people danced around the floor. School concerts three times a year were very popular. The pupils enjoyed showing off their skills as performers as they sang, danced and acted out mini dramas. Despite the fact that these performances were solely European-oriented, the children always enjoyed the audiences.

Instruction on survival skills and bushcraft remained a recreational activity. Whilst the speaking of traditional language was forbidden, and the women would never observe or participate in religious ceremonies, rites and rituals, the myths and legends would always be in their hearts and stored away in the back of their minds, awaiting that special moment when they would be recalled and passed on to others. To ensure this, Kate's substitute and surrogate mothers who gave her maternal protection became her tutors. The forbidden topics were whispered in hushed tones in the privacy of the dormitory in the evenings or discussed on the grassy banks near the river under the shade of the huge river gum.

Everyone was acquainted with all residents at the Settlement, so it was not uncommon to see groups of women and girls heading off in all directions to forage for berries, roots and tubers — this was a regular event every Saturday morning. It was almost a ritual when for at least once a week all females assumed their ancient roles as gatherers. The only difference now, however, was that women from the Kimberley, the Pilbaras and the Murchison were now gathering the traditional bush tucker of the Nyoongah people.

Every year between May and October djubak or karnoes

were dug. These were highly prized as a food source, some were the size and shape of new potatoes. Bohn or borna, a small, red, sometimes hot root was plentiful, as were other smaller tubers and roots. Berries of all shapes and sizes grew in abundance — and had names like emu berries (their shape and colour were like emu eggs), gold swan, crown wooley and the largest of all, the sand-plain berries. They were the size of an oval-shaped grape. Nuts and seeds were gathered and shared amongst the inmates.

During the summer months there were plenty of fish in the river, lonkies or wheppies and buguinge mud fish, and cobblers, and gilgies.

The men and boys hunted for small game such as rabbits, porcupines and parrots and galahs. The camp people who lived some 300 yards from the compound kept kangaroo dogs bred specially for hunting kangaroos and emus.

Family picnics or "dinner outs" were held on Sundays. Adults were queued up outside the kitchen servery counter to be given cardboard boxes of food. The contents were nearly always the same, mutton chops, bread, jam or golden syrup, tea, sugar and tinned milk. The men "robbed" bee hives and collected the wild honey while the women and children fished, dug gilgies (small freshwater crayfish) or caught lizards and cardars (goannas).

Local bush foods were not the only things to be introduced to the people of the north by the traditional owners of this part of the country, the Nyoongahs. They also shared their myths and legends. There were warnings not to wander off in the bush alone or go too far away, for behind every Christmas or Moodgah tree a berrijal or a charnock may be lurking. Malevolent spirits such as mummaries or wood archies preyed on disobedient children who have not heeded warnings of the grown-ups and are caught wandering home at dusk or night fall.

"When we came to a Moodgah tree at dusk we'd join

hands and run fast as we could. Don't you worry, fear would boost your speed up one hundred percent," said Kate.

"When we went on these Sunday 'dinner outs', it was better to take as many children as you can — you got more food. We enjoyed the weekends very much and looked forward to them. No child was an orphan then.

"But one thing I shall fear and remember always is the mournful cry of the curlew or weelow. We were told that the bird was imitating the cry of a tormented, demented woman searching for her lost children," said Kate shivering slightly. "I never forgot that legend."

Two years later the government decided that Kate and the other children would enter a new phase in their lives. It was time to abolish the protection policy and legislate a new policy — the assimilation policy. Basically the assimilation policy meant that Aborigines were expected to achieve and attain the same standards of living as their white counterparts, and they would eventually become absorbed into the mainstream Australian society and be treated equally as Australian citizens. The Settlements were closing down, becoming obsolete, and Christian missions were being established throughout the state under various denominations.

The Mission

We didn't travel down directly to the Roelands Native Mission Farm but made a couple of detours because the mission authorities were unsure whether they could take the full quota. They needed a fortnight to plan and reorganise themselves. So for two exciting weeks we holidayed in Perth at what was then the Displaced Persons Camp (for refugees from Europe) at Swanbourne. It seemed an appropriate place for a vacation — to us at least — the displaced and misplaced children from the Settlements.

The Displaced Persons from Europe, or DPs our guardians called them, and the misplaced children of Aborigines had little or no contact with each other. We were aware that these "New Australians" lived on the other side of the camp. All the girls were cautioned and instructed on what action to take if confronted by one: "Don't talk to them. Run straight to the huts immediately." Basically our fears and those of the staff had no foundation whatsoever. They were based purely on assumptions that these foreigners were all bad people, the worst kind of human beings on earth.

I can remember the first time I encountered one of them. It was one morning towards the end of our vacation. I was standing on the edge of the road watching intently for the girls to return from the canteen down the road.

They were bringing some P.K. and spearmint chewing gum and lollies. The girls from Moore River took to the chewing gum instantly, it was much more pleasant and enjoyable than the "bush chewies" we got from the gum or resin found on young banksias. We chewed these long after the flavour had gone.

I heard or at least I thought I heard a man's voice; it sounded very close. I turned quickly to face the speaker and there he was. A DP. An Eye talian (Italian) standing there grinning widely, displaying his discoloured tobacco-stained teeth. I forgot the chewing gum and ran like a frightened rabbit, and didn't stop until I was safely inside the hut.

Apart from such surprises those weeks in Perth were filled pleasantly sight-seeing, picnicking on the Swan River, Kings Park, visiting the South Perth zoo and going to the local picture theatres.

But swimming in the ocean was what we enjoyed the most — especially when we were being dumped by the big waves. We laughed at and with each other when we coughed, spluttered and blew our noses and went back for more. This was the first time we had seen the sea and found it most fascinating and enjoyable.

On the last day of our holidays we said our tearful goodbyes to our Roman Catholic friends who departed on a big bus to their final destination, the Wandering Mission near Narrogin. We wondered if we would ever meet again.

A further delay — the mission needed two more weeks, so we passed the time at the Carrolup Settlement waiting patiently for them to decide how many girls they were prepared to take in their charge. They said they would accept all of us Church of England girls.

· · · · ·

The first thing I noticed when we arrived at the entrance to the mission was the very large sign that said "The Roelands Native Mission Farm", and written underneath that was a text from the bible saying "Suffer the little children to come unto me and forbid them not for theirs is the Kingdom of God."

However, before we could be welcomed and accepted into the Kingdom of God we had to go through a cleansing process. First there was the bodily cleansing. Our long hair was shorn from above the ears, almost shorter than the boys at the mission. Nine years old, I bawled my eyes out as I watched my beautiful long tresses fall on to the floor in an untidy heap amongst the others. Then came the delousing process where our heads were saturated with kerosene. I hated that, the smell was enough to knock you out. The head lice had no chance of survival in those fumes.

This was followed by a hot bath with disinfectant in it — Dettol I think.

With the bodily cleansing completed, we were taken to our dormitories and introduced to our fellow inmates.

There were twenty girls whose ages ranged from five to fourteen, some from Carrolup Settlement (later known as the Marribank Mission) near Katanning, south of Perth, and the rest of us from Moore River Native Settlement.

We were labelled the "new girls", which only served to alienate us and cause rivalry between us and the "old girls", and we felt discriminated against because we were not "born again" Christians.

The environment at Roelands Native Mission Farm was totally different from Settlement conditions. The buildings were always clean and sparkling — almost sterile in fact — with the highly polished floors, the snow-white sheets, table cloths, and curtains in the dining room, with the fruits of the spirit sewn in green cotton on the frills. There was Faith, Hope, Love, Peace and Joy. Everywhere and everything about the place gave it an air of godliness, and righteousness prevailed.

The missionaries' aim was to save souls — and the business of saving our souls began in earnest. Our guidance through the paths of righteousness began with religious instruction that immediately took precedence over normal education. Our education in a fundamentalist religious indoctrination introduced us to the Christian virtues, principles and behaviour.

These missionaries believed in the literal translation of the bible, baptism and the power of prayer and the Holy Spirit. Their religion had no room for Aboriginal religion, Aboriginal customs and Aboriginal culture. Stronger criticisms reinforced the superstition and fear of our traditional culture. The colonial terms such as "uncivilised" and "primitive" were replaced with Christian terminologies. "Evil", "devil worshippers" and the "powers of darkness" were used when referring to Aboriginal culture.

This kind of indoctrination served only to widen the already established gulf between the traditionally-oriented and the ruralised Aborigines.

*   *   *   *   *

Within two or three years the missionaries had achieved their aim, many of us were converted and became born again Christians. We could memorise portions of the bible and learnt to identify quotes, texts and characters of the bible.

I believe it was through the continuous indoctrination of the Christian morality and tenets — and the constant warnings of the "wages of sin" and "wrath of God" — that all of us tried diligently and faithfully to stay on the path of righteousness and never stray off it.

With this new belief came even more heroes — though

this time they were biblical. These heroes were different from the previous ones, they were real, and seemed to be either punished severely for wrong-doings or highly praised and rewarded for their achievements — always about the good and the evil.

As our Christian education progressed, our formal education fell behind the rest of the state school system. With no formal education there were no formal examinations. Whilst we made satisfactory progress and advancement in the Christian faith, we gained no further knowledge of the world in the class at the little schoolhouse on the hill.

The teacher who taught the upper primary level was unqualified. A former Yorkshire grocer, Mr Bennett should have been called "Mr Long", because all he seemed to know about maths was long division, long multiplication and long addition. His talent as an organist and musician far exceeded his skills as a teacher of the three Rs.

His wife instructed the girls in needlework and embroidery. We learnt and sang a lot of hymns, English ballads or some folk songs from the British Isles.

In the mid 1950s the education of the children was taken over by the government — the department of education. Thus once again those of us who had a fondness for different or special subjects and the desire to excel in something — even though it may have been only to please the teacher — sat eagerly and ready to absorb whatever knowledge was being imparted.

Our newness became tarnished somewhat as we settled and became accepted and recognised as "the mission kids".

Seasonal Changes

My first impression of Roelands Mission was a favourable one — except for the slightly claustrophobic feeling the closeness of the hills induced. There were seven hills surrounding the mission, someone informed us. In fact "Seven Hills Mission", was its original name.

The landscape and the environment were peaceful and tranquil — even though it was a hot dry mid-summer's day and the paddocks were covered with dry grass and patches of bare brown dusty earth. I just knew that I was going to like living here.

It was paradise compared with the Settlement conditions. The food was wholesome and nutritious. An established vegetable garden, the mixed orchard that produced an abundance of stone fruits, apples, pears and citrus fruits, and eggs and dairy products, enabled the mission to be a self-supporting, productive and enterprising institution.

When winter came shrouded in its dismal grey mantle, the trees that were covered in the warm autumn coloured leaves now stood stark bare and leafless — almost lifeless. The playing fields were a slushy quagmire with springs of fresh water seeping through the ground. A cold and sombre atmosphere permeated the mission. The inmates stayed indoors — only venturing outside to perform rostered duties, attend school and to have our meals. The river had swelled and was spilling over its banks and the creeks were full and running down to join the river. The meeting of the waters took place at the fertile triagular plot where the vegetable garden was established.

The bullfrogs croaked very loudly in various tones all night. During the day we searched for these creatures, these croaking nuisances, to rid ourselves of their nightly plunk-plunking forever. We never found too many — a couple I think. So for the rest of the winter we either grew accustomed to their croaking or if you were one of the lucky ones you slept through it.

Rising early each morning when the mists were stationary over the river at sunrise was something you got used to. We braved the chilly frosty mornings to do our duties. It seemed that every movement every action was done mechanically, with no pleasure and definitely no enthusiasm.

It is needless to say that when spring came it was welcomed with opened arms. The landscape was transformed once again, and it stimulated the senses with the abundance of fragrance, colour and appeal.

With the sensation of spring one could easily become intoxicated by the blossoms, the flower gardens and the sight of the blaze of colour the golden wattle trees produce. There are seven varieties located around the mission. This is the time when the orchards are also filled with the abundance of blossoms which will later bear fruit.

In the fields of lush green pastures, the sheep and horses and cattle are grazing heavily. The unfurrowed fields are now covered with golden dandelions and white patches of subterranean clover. Spring is life, movement and productivity.

But if you were to ask any ex-mission boy or girl what they remember most specifically about the mission, they would probably say the hard work, discipline and the bible. And spring. The arrival of the grapefruit season meant the hard work of picking, washing and packing, ready to meet the demands of not only the local markets but overseas to Singapore. This was a busy time for us. Walnuts must be picked, washed and laid to dry. There was fruit to pick, to be preserved and to be made into jam.

Many may view this as a form of child labour but we didn't, we saw this as a labour of love. I suppose we felt obligated — after all we were family and we all benefited in the end.

It was easy to sing songs of praise about creation and life. And when I recall nostalgically my childhood experiences I will always remember these seasonal changes and also the other changes they bring with them, such as the change of pace, mood and concepts.

We looked forward to the long walks in the bush during the warm spring weather, when we feasted our eyes on the masses of wild flowers that grew in profusion west of the mission. There were splashes of colour and brilliance everywhere. It seemed as if every available space had become part of nature's beautiful garden; this parkland unspoiled and undisturbed by man. There were patches of light blue leschenaultia, and for contrast there were small bushes of violet blue hovea flowers and as always a carpet of white, pink and yellow everlasting. Scattered amongst the black boy rushes and under the huge gum trees a variety of bush orchids grew, displaying their exquisite beauty in varying colours for bushwalkers and nature lovers to admire and enjoy. We were discouraged from picking the flowers, though occasionally we were given permission to pick small posies to take back home to our dormitory to put in our commonroom.

In Autumn we sometimes emerged from the river banks with coronets of white bush clematis, which we named bridal creepers, and carried bouquets of white lillies. With garlands of these pretty white creepers trailing everywhere we dusky barefooted maidens paraded and danced amid the laughter and cheers. We were celebrating the innocence of youth and the emergence of romantic fantasies. Many of us declared that we would wear the same bridal creepers in our hair and carry lillies on our wedding day. We were going to be Easter brides.

So despite the rigid formality of the place, the prayers, the restrictions, and the narrow-minded Christian fundamentalist teachings — the place, the location, will always be for me the embodiment of security, stability, peace and tranquility.

The Separation

Special friendships were formed there. In our case there was me, Kate Muldune 17 years, Melanie Jones 16 years, Kathy Williams 16 years, and Aileen Miles 14 years. We were a champion tennis squad, and were always on the same side in team sports such as netball and hockey. We worked, played, and moved as a team. Then one day without any explanation we were all separated. I was sent to Dorrington in the central wheat belt to work as a domestic help to Bill and Betty Hammond. Melanie and Kathy went south to Donnybrook and Busselton and the youngest member of the foursome, Aileen, remained to attend the Bunbury Senior High School.

At the time I couldn't understand the reason for our separation. It became obvious in later years but I could only guess at this stage. In those days our special friendship was viewed in a different light. Our relationship (their interpretation) was perhaps leaning towards lesbianism. But how could we have known about homosexuality when we were ignorant of the facts of life anyway. That assumption was absolutely ridiculous. The only reference to actual sexual relationship was made in the bible — describing the action as "he/she lay with her/him". Laying or lying meant to us the act of reclining. How, where or why didn't interest or concern us at all.

Even girls who planned a career in nursing were ignorant and naive as well. The reproductive system wasn't included in the Health, Hygiene and Physiology course studied by them. So it wasn't surprising that Beth Keeley, a first year student nurse at the Royal Perth Hospital, became alarmed when a male patient indicated that he was sexually aroused. The sister-in-charge of that particular ward was astonished as she looked at this attractive nineteen year old nurse with disbelief. After revealing her sheltered background, the sister understood and arranged for her to attend a lecture and film on reproduction. At least she was enlightened without having to learn from practical experience — by trial and error from boyfriends or husbands.

The Crossroads

It wasn't until several years later that the negative effects of my Christian fundamentalist education, values and attitudes became apparent. Both incidents were most traumatic and devastating.

The first incident occurred when I met my father Danny Atkinson, my stepmother Winnie, sisters Janey and Lizzy and baby brother Robert for the first time. The meeting took place on Mt Ross Station, two hundred miles northeast of Kingsley. My surrogate mother Josie Mayler (nee Leach) accompanied me and my four children to the station to explain the customs and instruct me on traditional and social behaviour.

"All the people who have settled at the Jigalong Mission have either been given anglo names or have had their Aboriginal names anglicised for identification purposes. Your Dad's surname is Atkinson now," Josie explained.

"They seemed to have used all the letters in the alphabet except X, Y and Z," she added.

Throughout my life all reference to Aboriginal tribal, traditional culture had been negative and adverse. So it was with fear, trepidation and curiosity that I allowed myself to be led to my father's camp. That thick impregnable wall erected by the colonists and Christianity had crumbled and I was actually coming face to face with people who were once described to me as "devil worshippers".

Before the meeting I was like the hundreds of other European-oriented Aborigines, those without a tradition or a past, those who had undergone (successfully I might add) conditioning to lose our memories of our families and heritage. Those negative beliefs have been firmly ingrained and imbedded forever. That invisible barrier — the gulf between the fullblooded Aborigine and the half-caste created by the colonials and widened by the Christians was a permanent fixture.

The confusion and conflict arose not from the actual contact with my family, but from confronting the negative and adverse aspects of Aboriginal culture. "Devil worshippers" and "primitive savages". These descriptions of the traditionally-oriented Aborigines kept bouncing around in my head. I couldn't could get rid of them, even when our visits to the station became annual or later bi-annual events and the children learnt to recognise all the local "bush tucker" and became more interested and involved in their traditional heritage. My children were not only learning to recognise bush foods but used the traditional names in Mardu Wangka, such as minyara (wild onions), kulyu (wild sweet potato), quomalla (wild tomato) and murrundu (goanna).

I refused to even attempt to repeat any Mardu words, that would surely indicate that I was allowing myself to be influenced and controlled by a people and a system of beliefs that was destructive and dangerous. I and or rather my mind rejected anything traditionally Aboriginal — except the food — and that included the language, the culture and especially its ceremonies, rites and rituals.

What a pathetic, misguided, misinformed woman I was then. Here I was unjustly condemning a culture that had survived and practised for over 40,000 years. It took almost ten years to undo the damage caused by foreign indoctrination and shake off the shroud of fear and superstition.

How could I despise my own flesh and blood, and how could I not love this warm, caring man who calls me "my gel" and who proudly introduces me to his friends and acquaintances as "my daughter". All my life I have always had substitute or surrogate mothers — but I have never called any other man "dad". There were many uncles but only one dad. I realise now that I have a past, a history that I have become extremely proud of. I even have a genuine skin name. I am a Milangga, the same skin section as my grandmother Lucy Muldune. This is my birthright and no one can take this away from me.

· · · · · ·

I am pleased to say that attitudes towards Aborigines have changed. Their culture, and especially their art and dances, are accepted and enjoyed all over the world. Aboriginal people everywhere are making sojourns to their traditional land, searching for their roots, their history and their heritage.

One thing I find most interesting is that with the resurgence of the popularity and the spreading of Aboriginal culture, many well-known Aboriginal identities have gone to the extent of adopting traditional Aboriginal names, proudly announcing to the world that they have a heritage, a history, and are proud to be recognised as an Australian Aborigine.

There were quite a few children like myself who never forgot some special words. Those in authority were successful in changing our attitudes towards Aboriginal culture. Yet they couldn't remove the words. The words stayed with us. Words remained in our sub-conscious mind despite the intensive conditioning by those in authority. Mardu words such as marmu (devil) and marlba, meaning malevolent spirits, and mabarn, a term used to describe the Mardu doctor or medicine man. Or it can be any objects that have magical powers to heal, recover lost property and avenge those who have harmed you.

The word mabarn was recalled instantly when my stepmother Winnie mentioned in whispered tones that my father had to visit the Mabarn man. I understood exactly what she meant. Memories of a cold, blustery, windy day at the camps at the Moore River Settlement came flooding back. My friend Shirley Riley and I (both seven or eight at the time) were taken out to dinner by Shirl's married sister Nora Walton. Two chooks were killed and cleaned for the occasion, and we were given a giblet each. We were absolutely delighted when we saw the unusual geometrical design on them. We rushed to the nearest shrubs where we dug holes and buried them. "This gunna be our mubarns eh Kady," Shirley said seriously. I nodded in agreement as we returned to the camp. The aroma of curried chicken floated towards us.

"Where are those giblets you girls? Bring them here, I want to clean and cook them for yous now," Nora told us.

"… Clean …", "… cook …." We looked at each other across the open fire. Shirley was pouting in disappointment, mirroring my feelings exactly, for in that moment all our hopes of obtaining magical powers vanished immediately.

I am pleased that those years of fear and uncertainty are behind me now and my knowledge of my traditional culture is constantly expanding. Although I don't participate in the religious activities, I am well aware of their significance and also of the roles the participants play in them. As a family member I can choose whether to become involved or to remain a casual observer. I now converse and communicate in Mardu Wangka and listen more intently as the Dreamtime stories are told so that I can share them with my children and grandchildren. This is my heritage, this is theirs too.

• · · • •

It wasn't until after my marriage to Kent Williamson, the handsome, charming, garrulous man with wavy auburn coloured hair and the mischievous green eyes, that I began to question the relevance of my Christian values and how to apply them in a negative situation such as a marriage breakdown. Ideally we weren't supposed to fall out of love, under any circumstances.

I fell in love with him when I saw him lying on his side chewing on a stalk of a yellow sour grass plant. It was there I perceived and desired the man of my dreams. There could be no one else. On that day on Bill and Betty Hammond's farm east of Dorrington, youth and spring had all the ingredients to nurture and develop into a full blown romance.

I still have visions (though they are vague) of the vivacious self-confident young woman full of gaiety and expectation of love, sitting on a large grey rocky granite — my special place — sharing this lovely view with this handsome young man at my side.

Beauty and colour were everywhere, in every direction as far as the eyes could see. The farm in the springtime was beauteous, bountiful and blessed and Dorrington was unforgettable. Spread out all around us was a gigantic patchwork quilt of nature: the verdant green fields of wheat, barley and oats, paddocks of golden dandelions, the pale lemon-coloured sour grass plants, the pink, white and yellow everlastings covering every available space under the wattle thickets along the fences.

How many times had I stood on top of this rock and felt an uncontrollable urge to sing a certain hymn appropriate for the mood and sight. It was a favourite song of everyone.

> There is spring time in my soul today,
> More glorious and bright

The little ones who didn't know the words of the verse would join in the chorus with gusto and enthusiasm.

> Oh there's sunshine, blessed sunshine,
> Where the peaceful happy moments roll,
> When Jesus shows his smiling face
> There is sunshine in my soul.

I felt like a mountain goat, surefooted, full of life and expectations. The world was at my feet.

Dressed in dark blue serge trousers and a red, black and white checked shirt, Kent Williamson tried desperately to convince me that sexual intercourse was a ritual, an act of love performed anywhere, at any time by a couple in love.

I reminded him that I grew up with rigid Victorian values and codes of behaviour reinforced by the bible. Warnings against human follies were strongly supported by adages, proverbs, texts and quotes from the bible. I never realised before that I had certainly lived a sheltered life.

"Go no further than kissing," warned Mrs Hammond. "Tell him that you'll accept nothing less than a wedding ring."

I heeded her advice and I never weakened.

Our marriage took place at the Dorrington Church of Christ, performed by the Rev. John Crowley. My matron-of-honour was my best friend Jane Walters, and my junior bridesmaid was Annette Hammond. Both wore ballerina length dresses of leschenault-blue organza with puffed sleeves, carrying bouquets of pink roses, and pink everlastings, and coronets of pink roses in their hair. I wore a traditional-length gown of white satin, and carried a bouquet of white roses, frangipani and white honeysuckle, and borrowed Mrs Hammond's long lace veil.

The groom, his best man and groomsman (his brothers Paul and Garry) wore pale grey suits, white shirts and blue ties. It was the happiest day of my life. I was given away by Mr Hammond, my boss and friend. The reception was held at the church hall and was attended by all of the Hammonds and all of the members of the Young Peoples Christian Endeavour Union. "A dry wedding," sniffed Sara Jane, Kent's mother, because no alcohol was served.

．．．．．

My heart was full of happiness as I accompanied my new husband back to settle in his hometown of Geraldton, a beautiful coastal town north of Perth. To me marriage was a goal achieved, a fulltime career and more importantly a sacred institution.

It was my fundamentalist Christian ideals that created so much confusion; its conflicting views and contradictions that caused my breakdown.

We have romantic role models for falling in love, those who have set the behavioural patterns for lovers, but there are no role models for getting out of love, are there?

You see, I couldn't understand, and I bewailed the fickleness of a man's love. For years I had to endure the selfishness of a charming husband who was unfaithful and disloyal at every opportunity.

What a trusting and naive wife I was then. Even when he didn't return home at the weekends. There was nothing mysterious with his absences, there was no need to be alarmed or concerned. His explanations and excuses were nearly always plausible. And besides he was always considerate and caring. I never doubted his word and accepted his denial of everything. Why shouldn't I, our marriage vows were sacred weren't they? Or so I thought.

As the years rolled by, things got worse, his attitude towards me changed drastically. I found myself contending with unfair condemnation, cursing and swearing, using descriptions and vile names I never heard in my entire life.

I had to endure barbed remarks which were just as painful as physical violence. These attacks came at regular intervals. There were insulting accusations implying that I had slept with every man I had any kind of contact with.

My mother-in-law Sara Jane's behaviour was no better. She was a vicious and vindictive woman. I never understood why I was singled out as her victim to humiliate and intimidate. Perhaps it was my Christian upbringing that was my downfall. "Respect your elders," we were taught — even when they didn't deserve it. My attitude must have been interpreted as meekness, and I was a person "to be set upon". "Condone their follies, forgive their faults." It was easy to be rhetorical and sit in judgment from afar but what was I meant to do, suffer humiliation "until death do us part"?

No way. If I am to be restored to a strong individual, a woman in my own right, I need to grab with both hands the separation that is offered. There is no hope of reconciliation. I know now he is incapable of remaining devoted to me, I must accept that and pick up the pieces, care for and love my children and start a new life. I have resolved never to get involved with anyone again, though I still have the unconscious desire to be appreciated and loved.

Holding steadfast to my Christian beliefs almost ruined my life. I was fast becoming a neurotic woman addicted to Valium. I was rescued from this fate by some strong and practical advice from my dearest friend and matron-of-honour at my wedding, Jane Walters.

"Go back to study. Do something different," she advised.

I took her advice and enrolled at the Geraldton Technical College and faced the most difficult challenge of my life. For a middle-aged woman whose formal education never passed the primary stage, this task was daunting.

Two years later I applied and was accepted as a student with the Aboriginal Bridging Course at the Western Australian Institute of Technology. Kent couldn't resist the temptation. He just had to call in just as we were about to leave for Perth. "You'll never make it. You're too dumb," he said.

Midway through the course I was almost convinced that he was right. But I wasn't giving him the pleasure of saying "I told you so". I may have lacked confidence at times but not stamina, persistence and determination.

• • • • •

And so with my friend David Larsen's support and encouragement I took advantage of the means of study and I was able to complete the Aboriginal Bridging Course successfully.

My first contact with David Larsen was at the official welcoming ceremony for the incoming students. Regular interaction and socialisation between the tertiary and the ABC students on the campus brought us together often. I felt comfortable with this quiet, sensitive caring man. He wasn't as handsome as Kent Williamson. He was average looking, fair haired, tall and slender, but he had other qualities that I admired in a man. He was the grandson of a Danish sojourner from Copenhagen. Father of three grown-up children, he was divorced from his wife because life with him was "dull and boring". His interests were reading, films and fishing. At that stage in my life I was convinced that I had become frigid and unable to share an intimate relationship. I was content to leave things as they were, sharing friendship and companionship.

The Graduation

It was 4 o'clock in the afternoon and the heat was unbearable, so still and sweltering. The Fremantle Doctor was late coming in as usual. I had planned to sleep through it, but my three boisterous grandsons decided otherwise. There was only one place left where I could relax and reflect on events and incidents of the past year, and that was the bathroom.

So for the next twenty minutes I soaked in a tepid bath undisturbed.

Three years ago the chances of furthering my education were so remote that even doing a course at a TAFE college seemed highly unlikely. Yet here I am on this hot November afternoon preparing for a very special evening — the graduation ceremony of the Aboriginal Bridging Course students 1981 at the Western Australian Institute of Technology. There are eighteen graduates, sixteen women and only two men; the females outnumber the males once again. This is a statement in itself and one that should dispel the myth that has persisted throughout the decades that women are merely "breeders, feeders and follow the leaders". We see ourselves as strivers and survivors. Our contribution not only to Aboriginal society but to the wider community is well documented. Women hold prominent positions and are attaining increasingly important roles in administration at all levels in welfare, education, business and the arts.

There are a few students like myself still suffering low self-esteem and the effects of traumatic experiences. A couple of students who have had little or no contact with Aboriginal people were going through an identity crisis. Thankfully, all these problems have been overcome and adjustments made by the end of the course. I readily adjusted to city life but found it extremely difficult being a fulltime mature-aged student on a tertiary campus. But persistence and determination paid off in the long run. All the study and hard work had come to fruition, and I want to look my best this evening.

Later as I sat at my dresser the reflection in the mirror showed a fairly attractive woman with careworn lines around the eyes and greying around the temples. A grandmother of forty-one years, this woman with dark neatly trimmed hair brushed up into a flattering style. It was normally straight, thick and lacked lustre. But today it was glossy and seemed to make my dark eyes look brighter. Later when my daughter Vicki completed the facial makeup, she stood back and surveyed her handiwork. She nodded, satisfied with the results, "Mum you look different, beautiful in fact. A little bit of makeup, a bit of colour here and there, especially mauves and blues really suits you, you should wear it often."

I was flattered. I have never worn makeup before. My Christian principles disallowed and discouraged with adages such as "A little bit of powder, a little bit of paint, makes a lady what she aint."

When David Larsen, my companion and escort, called to pick me up, I could see that he approved of my new image — my glamorous, flattering appearance

"Gee, Kate you look lovely," he said.

I am glad I chose to wear the mauve and white suit

with matching white shoes. I felt all bubbly and beautiful as we drove to the campus at Bentley.

The day that I strived for these past three years had finally arrived. And as I took my place in the second row with my fellow graduates, the class of '81, I became acutely aware of the ambience — an atmosphere filled with nervous anticipation and excitement that seemed to permeate the entire length and breadth of the Hollis Theatre.

However, my nervousness and anxiety quickly disappeared as I stepped on to the podium to receive a handshake and a certificate from the dean of the faculty of education.

This ceremony may have been regarded by a few as just another graduation ceremony: a presentation of rhetorics and concluding with the usual congratulatory speeches, followed by a vote of thanks and an invitation to share refreshments at the main cafeteria. But to me the ceremony signified something special. It meant that I had reached yet another goal in my life — a personal achievement worth sharing with an audience — one that I had doubted I would ever attain. Seated amongst the audience, sharing this special moment with me were my four very proud children, their spouses and my five grandchildren.

Firstly there was my eldest child Kevin James, 21, a plant operator with Carnarvon Shire Council, and his attractive wife Helen and their two sons Richard, 3, and Paul, 1.

Next to them were my daughter Vicki, 19, clerk/typist with the Department of Social Security, Cannington, her husband Marty Harris, trainee welfare assistant at a juvenile centre, and their sons Peter, 5, and Shane, 4.

Marise my youngest daughter came down from Port Hedland with her handsome husband Johnny Morgan and my only and beautiful granddaughter Jasmine, 3. At

17 Marise still looked too young to be a mother — just a baby herself.

Kent, the baby of the family, a sixteen-year-old apprenticed motor mechanic, intended joining his father and uncles on the Main Roads Board (Murchinson Area) when he qualified.

With the formalities over, the refreshments devoured and enjoyed, everything was going perfectly. There were more congratulatory hugs and kisses from fellow students, family and friends. But my highest accolade came from my eldest son Kevin James who waved and yelled before disappearing around the corner, "Well done Mother duck, we're all proud of you." I was proud of me too, the only grandmother in the class.

That evening was still mine, as my friend David cheerfully reminded me. Next on the agenda was a celebration party at Dulcie Miller's home in Como. Dulcie was a second year social work student — the same year as my friend David — and she was the most helpful and popular person on campus. Many of us benefited from her support and informative discussions.

David and I didn't go directly to Como but drove to South Perth to the foreshore and sat on the edge of the river's cool grassy banks.

"I brought a bottle of champagne but forgot to bring two glasses," he said apologetically. "But I hope you don't mind using this." He handed me a small plastic bottle of orange juice.

Mind, I didn't mind at all — unromantic though it may seem. Starting off with an orange juice, followed by an orange and champagne cocktail and ending with champagne. It sounded perfectly wonderful to me.

Some time later David took the empties and deposited them into the nearest rubbish bin. I walked and stood on the edge of the foreshore and gazed wistfully across the river to the brightly lit city with its scores of twinkling lights and colourful neon signs that seem to enhance the beauty and the brilliance of our night-time capital city. I listened to the humming and the throbbing of the city itself, and watched the twin head lights of the moving traffic; going to and fro; in and out; full of purpose, either going home or going out.

This beautiful view was reflected in the river's edge on the opposite side. Though now the twinkling lights seemed to be multiplied many times to become streaks of brilliance and colour. The transformation was magical. The normally murky brown Swan River seemed to be momentarily transformed into a huge mirror. In the darkness the ripples and the low swell lapped against the shoreline, breaking and rejoining in an endless movement, never stopping, never still.

A cool breeze came wafting across the waters, giving me a pleasant feeling that was purely euphoric.

This entire evening's proceedings were a little hazy — except for three words that kept echoing in my brain, "Passed with distinction". And at that moment I realised the full impact of those words. I actually made it. You hear that, Kent Williamson, "Passed with distinction". It felt so good I wrapped my arms around myself, as pride and self-satisfaction began to swell within my breast. A most gratifying feeling indeed.

I was so engrossed in my own thoughts that I didn't hear David approaching until he put his arms around me and kissed my cheek. "Beautiful, eh," he said. I nodded in agreement and turned towards him and embraced and kissed him. But this time, however, it was different. I felt an old familiar emotion stirring within me; a sensation I thought was dead, gone forever, when all this time it was just lying dormant waiting for the right moment.

Well that special moment has come. Winter is over.

Spring is here. My spirits soar higher. I am alive! I am vibrant! I am Caprice, a Stockman's Daughter.

Black Australian Writing Series

Since 1988 with the establishment of the David Unaipon competition, which discovers new Aboriginal and Torres Strait Islander writers, UQP has built up an international reputation as the largest publisher of books by Indigenous authors in Australia. UQP's Black Australian Writing series evolved out of the Unaipon Award and today includes Indigenous-authored books ranging from novels, poetry, and life stories to nonfiction, and young adult fiction. Through the combined expertise of our authors, cultural advisors and specialist staff, UQP continues its commitment to Indigenous writing as a valued contribution to the literature of a nation.

Available in UQP's Black Australian Writing Series are:

DORIS PILKINGTON/NUGI GARIMARA
CAPRICE: A stockman's daughter

A fictional account of one woman's journey to find her family and heritage, *Caprice* is Doris Pilkington Garimara's first book. Set in the towns, pastoral stations and orphanage-styled institutions of Western Australia, this story brings together three generations of Mardu women. The narrator Kate begins her journey with the story of her grandmother Lucy, a domestic servant, then traces the short and tragic life of her mother Peggy.

Winner of the 1990 David Unaipon Award
ISBN 0 7022 3356 0
Fiction

DORIS PILKINGTON/NUGI GARIMARA
FOLLOW THE RABBIT-PROOF FENCE

'A marvellous adventure story and thriller, celebrating the courage and the resilience of the human heart.'

— Phillip Noyce, Director of 'Rabbit-Proof Fence'

This book is the basis of the internationally released film 'Rabbit-Proof Fence'. Based on her mother Molly's life story, Doris Pilkington Garimara's narrative tells of three young girls' remarkable journey home across the length of Western Australia.
ISBN 0 7022 3355 2
Non-fiction

VIVIENNE CLEVEN
HER SISTER'S EYE

Powerful and sinister, this is the second book by the brilliant Murri writer whose comedy novel *Bitin' Back* (2001) won the David Unaipon Award and was shortlisted in the 2002 South Australian Premier's Award for Fiction. Cleven's facility with noir is every bit as biting as her wit. *Her Sister's Eye* is a haunting descent into the tragedies of lives both black and white in a small town community with a legacy of shame.

ISBN 0 7022 3283 1

Fiction

VIVIENNE CLEVEN
BITIN' BACK

This is a rollicking comedy novel that blends in nimbly the realities of small town prejudice and racial intolerance. When football-playing Nevil awakens one morning determined to don a frock and "eyeshada" to better understand the late novelist Jean Rhys, his mother's idle days at the bingo hall are ended forever. Neither fist fights at the Two Dogs Pub, bare knuckle boxing in the back paddock, Booty's pig dogs or a police siege can slow the countdown on this human time bomb.

Winner of the 2000 David Unaipon Award

ISBN 0 7022 3249 1

Fiction

ROBERT LOWE
THE MISH

An award-winning story of family, community and tradition on Victoria's Framlingham Aboriginal Mission. *The Mish* is a charming, humorous memoir of times past, about growing up on western Victoria's Framlingham Aboriginal Station in the 1950s and '60s. Robert Lowe's family came to the Mission of their own volition at a time when mixed race marriages were better supported by the Aboriginal community than by the white community. A celebration of the resilient and unified extended family.

Winner of the 2001 David Unaipon Award

ISBN 0 7022 3327 7

Memoir